# SPACE JUNK

## THE DANGERS OF POLLUTING EARTH'S ORBIT

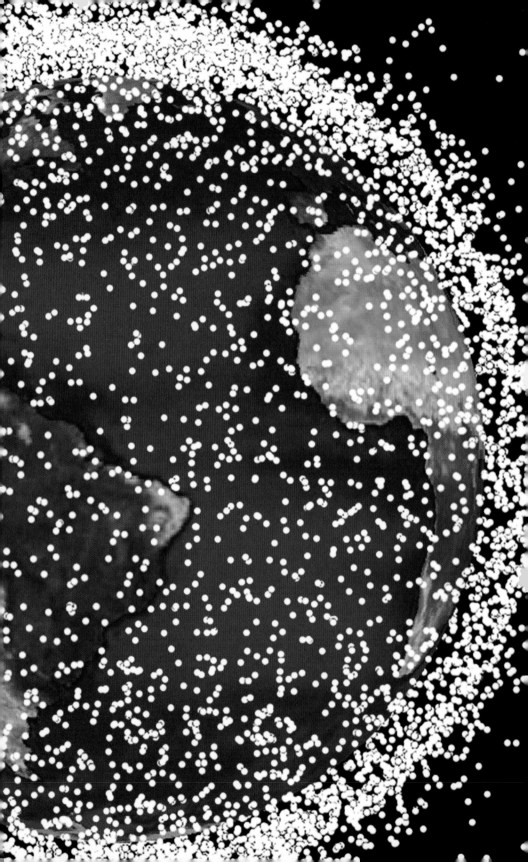

# SPACE JUNK

## THE DANGERS OF POLLUTING EARTH'S ORBIT

KAREN ROMANO YOUNG

TWENTY-FIRST CENTURY BOOKS / MINNEAPOLIS

For Ann with thanks.
Make like a satellite and stick around.

Twenty-First Century Books
A division of Lerner Publishing Group, Inc.
241 First Avenue North
Minneapolis, MN 55401 USA

For reading levels and more information, look up this title at www.lernerbooks.com.

Main body text set in Adrianna 10/16. Typeface provided by Chank.

**Library of Congress Cataloging-in-Publication Data**

Young, Karen Romano, author.
    Space junk : the dangers of polluting earth's orbit / Karen Romano Young.
        pages cm
    Summary: "This book examines the proliferation of space debris in outer space and discusses methods of retrieving and disposing of the material."— Provided by publisher.
    Audience: Ages 12–18.
    Audience: Grades 9 to 12.
    Includes bibliographical references and index.
    ISBN 978-1-4677-5600-6 (lb : alk. paper) — ISBN 978-1-4677-8806-9 (eb pdf)
    1. Space debris—Juvenile literature. 2. Space pollution—Juvenile literature. I. Title.
TL1499.Y68 2016
629.4'16—dc23                                                    2015013396

Manufactured in the United States of America
2-42476-17701-7/5/2016

# CONTENTS

Since the late 1950s, humans have launched thousands of objects into space. Some of them, like these Japanese craft (shown in an artist's rendering entering the atmosphere over South Australia), are designed to return to Earth. Others will drift in space until gravity and other forces pull them down.

# ZOMBIES IN SPACE

If we don't change the way we operate in space, all this results in an exponentially increasing amount of debris, until all objects are reduced to a cloud of orbiting fragments that are capable of destroying any spacecraft that attempts to operate anywhere within that cloud.

—*Donald Kessler, astrophysicist, 2014*

On February 10, 2009, high above Earth, two satellites slammed into each other. Both satellites were traveling at nearly 17,000 miles (27,350 kilometers) per hour when they crashed. One of the satellites—US communications satellite *Iridium 33*—had been going about its business. As it orbited Earth, 490 miles (790 km) above the ground, it relayed signals from one cell phone to another. With no warning, another satellite came barreling out of the dark. *Cosmos 2251,* a Russian communications satellite, had been launched into space in 1993 and had stopped operating two

years later. Unlike operational satellites, *Cosmos* was no longer under the control of people on Earth. It was orbiting on its own, circling Earth the same way Earth and the other planets circle the sun. Drifting off its original course, *Cosmos* sped into *Iridium*'s path. High above Siberia, part of northern Russia, the two spacecraft slammed into each other, smashing each other to smithereens. The two spacecraft broke apart into more than twenty-one hundred shards of metal, glass, plastic, and paint, which blasted out from the collision in every direction.

Satellites operated by Iridium Communications in Virginia relay signals from one cell phone on Earth to another. In 2009 a Russian zombie satellite (a satellite that is no longer functioning or controlled by people on Earth) smashed into an Iridium satellite. The two spacecraft broke apart into hundreds of pieces of metal, plastic, glass, and paint. Many Iridium customers lost phone service after the crash.

Most of this material is still orbiting Earth. And each piece— from fingernail-sized chips of paint to chunks of metal as big as a human head—has the potential to strike and damage other spacecraft. Eventually, through orbital decay, objects orbiting Earth will slow down and drop into the atmosphere, the layer of gases surrounding the planet. Most of these objects will burn up and disintegrate high in the air, but some pieces of debris could hit the ground, possibly hurting people, animals, or buildings.

## FROM SATELLITES TO SPACE JUNK

Since the late 1950s, humans have launched more than sixty-six hundred satellites into space. Some of these craft are as small as shoe boxes. Others are as big as school buses. Rockets carry them into space and then release them into orbit.

Each satellite is designed to do a specific job. Some satellites take images of Earth, the moon, and other objects in space. Others study weather and atmospheric conditions on Earth. Communications satellites relay TV, telephone, and radio signals from one location to another. Some nations use satellites to gather military intelligence, such as the location of ships and weapons depots in foreign countries. Commanded by people on the ground, satellites are equipped with computers, cameras, sensors, and other instruments. Rocket fuel, batteries, and solar panels provide them with the power they need to carry out their jobs and to travel through space.

Of the sixty-six hundred satellites launched into space since the late 1950s, about one thousand are still functioning, doing the jobs they were designed for. About three thousand of these satellites stopped operating at some point and eventually fell back to Earth, pulled down by orbital decay. Of this group, most completely burned up when they reentered Earth's atmosphere. But in a few cases, debris from falling satellites has hit the ground, although so far it hasn't caused any serious damage on Earth. The remaining twenty-six hundred nonoperational satellites are called zombies. Like *Cosmos 2251,* they are out of fuel and out of communication with Earth. But they will continue to orbit the planet until orbital decay pulls them down. (The higher they are in orbit, the longer they will remain in space.) The zombies are so numerous that they endanger new, functional satellites and other spacecraft.

Scientists use the term *space junk* to describe any human-made debris in space, from the tiniest pieces of metal to intact but nonoperational satellites. Zombie satellites are the largest pieces of space junk. Other large pieces include the upper sections of the rockets used to launch spacecraft into orbit. Smaller pieces of space junk include a glove that floated

## That Burning Feeling

When objects rub against one another, a natural force called friction slows them down. Friction also creates heat. When rockets boost satellites into orbit and when satellites fall out of orbit and reenter Earth's atmosphere, they rub against the air.

The friction that results makes the satellites extremely hot, sometimes causing them to burst into flames. The same thing happens when asteroids and meteors (chunks of metal and rock that fly through space) hit Earth's atmosphere.

Sailors from the USS *Anchorage* retrieved the National Aeronautics and Space Administration's Orion spacecraft *(top right)* following its splashdown in the Pacific Ocean in December 2014 after a two-orbit test flight. The sailors maneuvered Orion into a chamber at the bottom of the ship, which took the vehicle back to shore for reuse. Orion is used to carry astronauts into space and back.

Spacecraft that carry astronauts must be specially designed so that they don't get too hot when they exit and reenter Earth's atmosphere. Engineers outfit these vehicles with heat-reflecting tiles, insulation, and other equipment to keep them cool during exit and reentry. (Sometimes the tiles and other materials fall off during spaceflight, further adding to space junk.) Some spacecraft reentering the atmosphere are aimed to land in the ocean, which further cools them when they reach the surface of Earth.

away from astronaut Ed White in 1965, when he became the first American to walk in space; a tool kit that slipped from US astronaut Heidemarie Stefanyshyn-Piper's hand during a 2007 space walk; and the thousands of pieces of debris from the *Cosmos* and *Iridium* crash.

Without a powerful telescope, you can't see zombie satellites or any other space junk. But using high-tech equipment, scientists can detect and monitor space junk as it orbits. By 2011 scientists had identified twenty thousand pieces of junk in space, and they expect this figure to triple by 2030. But those

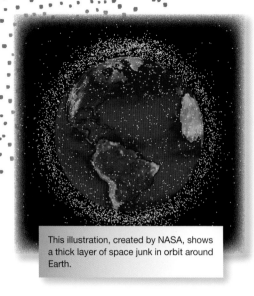

This illustration, created by NASA, shows a thick layer of space junk in orbit around Earth.

numbers represent only junk that's large enough to track. Tiny objects that can't be tracked from Earth probably number in the millions, according to scientists. And each piece of junk—from full-sized satellites to the tiniest shards of metal—has the potential to collide with other objects, blowing them to pieces and creating more junk. As the amount of junk in space increases, the likelihood of more collisions balloons.

"To get an idea of our current space environment, imagine this ball is our planet and this sand is space debris," said aerospace engineer Jonathan Missel, holding a beach ball in one hand and a small handful of sand in the other. "At first glance, you might think, yeah, there's a lot of stuff [space junk], but it's small and fairly spread out, and you'd be right in some ways. Full scale, the objects are usually farther apart than mountaintops [on Earth], so the chance of any two colliding at any given moment is pretty small. But they're all moving around in orbit, so as time passes the chances [of collision] build up, with every moment of every day of every year."

## EARLY SPACE EXPLORATION

The Space Age began on October 4, 1957, with the launch of *Sputnik 1*, the world's first human-made satellite. (Natural objects that orbit other bodies in space, the way the moon orbits Earth, are also called satellites.) Sent up by the former Soviet Union (a nation composed of Russia and fourteen other republics that existed from 1922 to 1991) to study Earth's atmosphere, the 23-inch-wide (58-centimeter) metal sphere burned up when it reentered the atmosphere three months after its launch.

*Sputnik* kicked off the space race between the United States and the Soviet Union, which were political, economic, and cultural enemies at the time. The two nations competed fiercely to outdo each other in many arenas, including space technology and space exploration. The United States launched its first satellite, *Explorer 1,* in 1958, the year after the *Sputnik 1* mission. In 1961 Soviet cosmonaut (Russian for *astronaut*) Yuri Gagarin, traveling in a craft called *Vostok,* became the first person to orbit Earth. Later that year, Alan Shepard became the first American in space. He traveled in a craft called *Freedom 7.* The first space junk also entered orbit in 1961. In June 1961, a rocket that had successfully launched a US military satellite called *Transit 4A* exploded in space. The rocket shattered into nearly three hundred pieces. Debris from the explosion is still in orbit.

In the early years of space exploration, scientists didn't worry about space junk. They believed in the big-sky theory that space was so enormous that any debris left there wouldn't interfere with operational spacecraft. So satellites were not designed to return to Earth when they had finished their jobs in space. They were simply left to drift. "We didn't think twice about [space junk]," says former astronaut Bryan O'Connor, who later became a safety officer with the US National Aeronautics and Space Administration (NASA).

## SPACE GETS MORE CROWDED

In the 1960s, as the Space Age took off, many nations began sending satellites into space. The United States and the Soviet Union also sent the first rockets to orbit the moon. The first humans to set foot on the moon were US

## Space Junk on the Moon

*Luna 2*, a Soviet craft that crash-landed on the moon in 1959, is still there. US lunar landers that carried Americans to the moon in the 1960s and 1970s remain there too, as do rovers that US astronauts drove over the moon's cratered terrain. Additional international space agencies have sent missions to the moon, and junk from these missions remains there as well. According to the *Atlantic* magazine, humans have left 400,000 pounds (181,400 kilograms) of material on the moon—equivalent to the weight of a Boeing 747. The junk includes seventy spacecraft; some TV, still, and film cameras; ninety-six bags of human waste; backpacks; twelve pairs of boots; empty space food containers; and two golf balls.

astronauts Neil Armstrong and Buzz Aldrin. They arrived with the US *Apollo 11* mission and stepped onto the lunar surface on July 20, 1969, while millions of people around the world watched the televised event. After this landing, the United States and other nations sent more missions to the moon. In the early 1970s, NASA began building the first US space station, called Skylab. Rockets carried the station into orbit in 1973. Skylab operated as a research station for astronauts for one year. After the astronauts left, Skylab continued on its normal orbit for four more years. It finally fell from orbit and broke apart as it reentered Earth's atmosphere in 1979.

Space shuttles are reusable craft that take off vertically like rockets and land horizontally like airplanes. The United States launched its first space shuttle in 1981. For the next thirty years, the five US space shuttles—*Columbia, Challenger, Discovery, Atlantis,* and *Endeavour*—carried people and equipment into space. For example, in 1990 *Discovery* carried the Hubble Space Telescope into orbit. The Hubble gathers images of distant space objects, such as stars, black holes, and far-off galaxies, and sends the images back to NASA, helping scientists learn more about deep space. Two space shuttles—*Challenger* and *Columbia*—malfunctioned during missions, killing all the astronauts on board. *Challenger* exploded shortly after launch in 1986, and *Columbia* broke apart as it reentered Earth's atmosphere in 2003. Because of safety concerns, cost, and the aging of its remaining shuttles, NASA retired the space shuttle fleet in 2011.

In 1998, building on the success of Skylab, a group of nations—including the United States, Russia, Canada, and Japan—began to build the International Space Station (ISS). Workers at NASA's Jet Propulsion Laboratory in California and at similar facilities around the world built sections of the station on Earth. Then space shuttles and other vehicles carried the pieces to the station site, where an international team of astronauts assembled the craft. Additional space stations that have launched since the ISS include Mir, a Soviet/Russian project that operated from 1986 to 2001.

Space exploration has continued into the twenty-first century. Space agencies around the world have sent numerous unpiloted spacecraft to study the sun, Mars and the other planets of the solar system, and space beyond the solar system. Among these spacecraft is *New Horizons,* a NASA probe that took off in February 2015. The probe will

An Atlas V rocket shot skyward from Vandenberg Air Force Base in California in 2013. The rocket carried NASA's Landsat Data Continuity Mission satellite, which photographs, measures, and monitors Earth's surfaces from space. Some sections of the rocket fell into the ocean after launch but others remain in orbit.

visit the dwarf planet Pluto and other objects in the Kuiper Belt, a region of orbiting bodies at the edge of the solar system. Then *New Horizons* will continue to travel outside the solar system.

In addition to sending probes to explore the solar system, humans continue to send satellites into orbit. More than fifty countries, as well as dozens of commercial businesses, educational organizations, and nonprofit groups operate these satellites. New satellites are launched at a rate of more than one hundred each year.

## OUT OF THIS WORLD

Different kinds of satellites travel along different orbits through space. Craft in low Earth orbit (LEO) are closest to Earth. They circle the planet at 112 to 1,242 miles (180 to 2,000 km) above Earth's surface. LEO is home to many satellites designed to monitor and track phenomena in the atmosphere, such as weather, or to photograph and monitor events on the ground, such as enemy military bases. The ISS also travels in LEO so that astronauts can reach it quickly. Astronauts sometimes need to service the Hubble Space Telescope, so it too orbits in LEO, with easy access from the ground. Some LEO satellites circle the planet directly above and along the equator, a geographical line around the center of Earth that is equidistant from the planet's two poles. Others travel perpendicular to the equator, moving around Earth from the North Pole to the South Pole and back again. Still other LEO satellites travel around the planet at an angle. The path a satellite takes is determined by the job it is designed to do.

Above LEO is mid-Earth orbit (MEO). Satellites in MEO are between 1,243 and 22,233 miles (2,000 and 35,780 km) above Earth. The farther an object is from Earth, the longer it takes to

## The International Space Station (ISS)

The largest craft in orbit around Earth, the ISS weighs nearly 1 million pounds (450,000 kg). Measuring 358 by 240 feet (109 by 73 meters), it is as long as a football field and 1.5 times as wide. The ISS is the third-brightest object in the sky (after the sun and the moon). If you know where and when to look, you can sometimes see the ISS from the ground without a telescope. To find out exactly when the ISS will be visible in the sky above your city, visit Spot the Station, a NASA website (http://spotthestation.nasa .gov), and use the Location Lookup tool.

The station cost more than $100 billion to build. Fifty-two computers aboard the ISS are used to control its operations. Astronauts who live onboard the ISS (sometimes for as long as a year) use it as a research laboratory. There, they study Earth, the solar system, and space. They also conduct experiments on how spending time in space affects living things. In fact, astronauts can feel these effects on their own bodies. For instance, they frequently suffer from stuffy noses, because out in space, gravity isn't strong enough to pull body fluids toward their feet, the way it would on Earth. Their faces also puff up with extra fluids, creating what's called a moon face.

circle the planet. So satellites in LEO will speed by a particular spot on Earth quickly, while those in MEO will remain overhead longer. Communications satellites and global positioning system (GPS) satellites (used to help people locate their precise locations on Earth) need this longer "dwell time" over certain regions and are therefore located in MEO.

A high Earth orbit (HEO) is more than 22,233 miles (35,780 km) above Earth. Some satellites in HEO move in an elliptical, or oval, orbit. These satellites pass close to Earth on one end of the oval and move far from Earth at the other end. Satellite operators use this orbit to view far northern or far southern parts of the planet. For instance, an elliptical orbit might take a satellite far into space above the North Pole but very close to Earth near the South Pole. Since the satellite is north of Earth for a long time as it travels, it gives operators on the ground an extended view of Earth's northernmost regions.

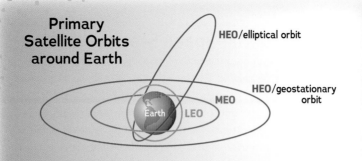

**Primary Satellite Orbits around Earth**

HEO/elliptical orbit

HEO/geostationary orbit

MEO

Earth

LEO

**LEO: low Earth orbit:** 112 to 1,242 miles (180 to 2000 km) above Earth

**MEO: mid-Earth orbit:** 1,243 to 22,233 miles (2,000 to 35,780 km) above Earth

**HEO: high Earth orbit:** more than 22,233 miles (35,780 km) above Earth

Other satellites in HEO travel in a geostationary orbit. Satellites in this orbit match Earth's counterclockwise rotation exactly, moving at the same speed at which Earth spins. As it moves in sync with Earth, a satellite in geostationary orbit can remain over one spot on the planet twenty-four hours a day. This positioning enables the craft to gather around-the-clock information on that spot. For instance, a satellite in geostationary orbit might monitor the weather nonstop in a single place on Earth.

## FLYING HIGH

Gravity is the naturally occurring force that keeps Earth circling the sun and keeps the moon circling Earth. Gravity also keeps satellites orbiting around Earth rather than flying off into space. In addition to being pulled by gravity, satellites also travel under their own power. Their power supplies, controlled by engineers on Earth, keep satellites orbiting at the correct distance above Earth and in the correct path, such as in an elliptical orbit.

The closer a satellite is to Earth, the stronger the pull of Earth's gravity. To counteract gravity, satellites need to travel very fast under their own power—and the lower the orbit, the higher the speed.

Satellites in low orbits can also be pulled to Earth by drag, a force that slows speeding objects. When a satellite travels through space, there is no air to slow it. But if the craft travels in the upper atmosphere, air can grab it the way wind grabs your hand when you stick it out of a car window. Drag can pull a satellite down or off course. That's another reason why satellites need their own power to stay in orbit.

Zombie satellites, on the other hand, have run out of fuel and have lost contact with controllers on Earth. They often orbit aimlessly and unpredictably, sometimes drifting into the paths of operational spacecraft. Without their own power, they cannot counteract the pull of gravity as they orbit Earth.

## Take It for a Spin

To understand the interaction between gravity and a speeding satellite, try this: Take a bucket of water outside. Hold it by the handle and spin around. Can you find the "sweet spot" where the water doesn't spill or splash but stays in the bucket as you spin it? The speed of your spin compares to the speed of a satellite orbiting Earth. If you slow down too much, the water will fall out, pulled to Earth by gravity. It's the same for a satellite. If it doesn't move quickly enough under its own power, it will start to fall back toward Earth.

## WHO'S IN CHARGE?

Within the United States, several organizations oversee satellites and other spacecraft. NASA controls human spaceflight and satellites involved in scientific space exploration. The US National Oceanic and Atmospheric Administration (NOAA) runs satellites that gather data about weather and the environment. The US Department of Defense (DoD) supervises

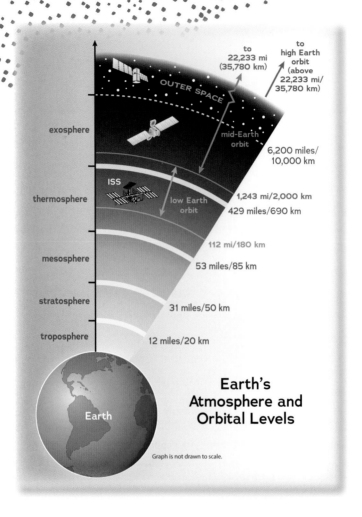

to
22,233 mi
(35,780 km)

to
high Earth
orbit
(above
22,233 mi/
35,780 km)

OUTER SPACE

exosphere

mid-Earth
orbit

6,200 miles/
10,000 km

ISS

thermosphere

low Earth
orbit

1,243 mi/2,000 km

429 miles/690 km

112 mi/180 km

53 miles/85 km

mesosphere

stratosphere

31 miles/50 km

troposphere

12 miles/20 km

Earth

**Earth's Atmosphere and Orbital Levels**

Graph is not drawn to scale.

satellites involved with the military and intelligence gathering. The US Federal Aviation Administration (FAA) oversees space tourism, an industry that is still in its early stages. The US Federal Communications Commission (FCC) is in charge of communications satellites. Other nations have similar organizations overseeing their own spacecraft and satellites. International groups such as the Committee on Space Research (COSPAR) bring together scientists to share the results of their research and to discuss issues related to space and to space travel.

National and international organizations work together to see that operational spacecraft stay on course and don't collide with one another. However, space is also filled with zombie satellites that are no longer controlled by people on Earth, as well as other space junk that was never under human control. These objects can make space travel treacherous. Scientists say that zombies come perilously close to operational satellites as often as fifteen hundred times a day.

Just what's up there? Scientists estimate that Earth's orbit holds one hundred million pieces of space junk measuring less than 0.4 inches (1 cm) and five hundred thousand pieces measuring 0.4 to 4 inches (10 cm). In addition, trackers on Earth have identified tens of thousands of objects the size of a coffee cup or larger. By the time you read this book, these numbers will have increased due to collisions between existing pieces of junk, which will result in more junk.

The layer of junk around Earth threatens to keep us grounded. If humans don't tackle the space junk problem, it might be impossible to leave the planet without being torn apart by flying metal. Humans would not be able to visit the moon, Mars, or other parts of the solar system. Space junk could trap us on Earth.

ESA's *Envisat*, shown here in an artist's rendering from 2002, became a zombie satellite when it stopped communicating with controllers on Earth in 2012. It is the biggest zombie in LEO.

# 2
# DEATH AND DESTRUCTION

The odds that you will be hit [by space junk] . . . are 1 in several trillion.

—Mark Matney, NASA Orbital Debris Program, 2011

In 2002 the European Space Agency (ESA, an organization with twenty European member nations) launched a school-bus-sized satellite called *Envisat*. Sailing through LEO, this big satellite studied Earth's land, ocean, ice caps, and atmosphere. In spring 2012, *Envisat* unexpectedly lost contact with controllers on the ground. A team of engineers tried to regain communication with the satellite, with no success. After a month, ESA gave up on *Envisat*. The satellite became LEO's largest zombie.

Engineers aren't sure why *Envisat* failed. A crucial piece of equipment on the satellite might have stopped working, or its electrical system might have short-circuited.

Satellites are complicated pieces of machinery, and any number of mechanical, electrical, or computer programs can disable them. Sometimes solar storms (huge bursts of energy from the sun) disrupt a satellite's electrical system, permanently cutting off communication with Earth. A collision with an existing piece of space junk might also disable a satellite. Often operators on the ground shut down satellites on purpose after their jobs in space are finished.

## CRASH COURSE

Satellites traveling under their own power can move at speeds of 4.3 to 5 miles (7 to 8 km) per second. That's 18,000 miles (28,968 km) per hour, almost seven times as fast as a speeding bullet. Even after a satellite becomes a zombie, it will continue to travel at high speed, although eventually gravity, drag, and friction will slow it down.

After two speeding objects collide in space, debris from the collision can shoot away from the blast even faster—at about 19,000 miles (30,577 km) per hour. The tiniest stuff moves fastest of all—up to 21,600 miles (34,760 km) per hour.

Astronauts retrieved solar panels from the Hubble Space Telescope in 2002 and brought them back to Earth. Engineers on the ground saw that the panels were full of dents and holes made by space debris.

Depending on the size and speed of objects that collide in space, the result can be like a bomb blast, with debris flying out in all directions. Such a collision can destroy a live satellite completely out of control. A powerful collision can knock a live satellite out of commission, off track, or into a descent.

The US space shuttles were frequently hit by space junk. In 1994 a paint chip hit the space shuttle *Endeavour* and made a dent that reached halfway through one of its windows. Had the window been broken, the astronauts on board could have been killed. In 2006 and 2007, debris blasted holes through radiators on both the *Atlantis* and *Endeavour* shuttles. The damage did not endanger the crews, although the radiators needed expensive repairs back on Earth.

In May 2009, NASA astronauts prepared to visit the Hubble Space Telescope for a repair mission involving five separate space walks (called EVAs, or extravehicular activities). Before the space shuttle *Atlantis* headed out to the Hubble, NASA engineers calculated the chance of the Hubble sustaining a "catastrophic" debris hit while the repair team was doing its work. The risk, according to the engineers, was 1 in 221. Compare that to your chances of dying in a plane crash, which are 1 in 11 million, to understand just how risky the mission was. Had the astronauts been hit by space junk, either out in space or while aboard *Atlantis,* the results could have been deadly. But the repair crew performed all five space walks and returned safely to Earth.

## DEBRIS DISASTER

While most collisions in space occur by accident, in 2007 China's space program purposefully created a crash to test a missile system. Governments don't want satellites from other nations snooping on their military operations from space, although this is common practice in the twenty-first century. So China created a

# Uncontrolled Entry

Space junk is not the only material that routinely slams into Earth's atmosphere. Asteroids and meteors do as well. On February 15, 2013, a 56-foot-wide (17 m) meteor plummeted through the atmosphere at 40,000 miles (64,375 km) per hour. It exploded 14 miles (23 km) above and 25 miles (40 km) south of the Russian city of Chelyabinsk. The explosion created a shock wave, a strong burst of air that circled the globe twice. In Chelyabinsk, the burst shattered windows, blew out doors, and blasted people off their feet. More than one thousand people were hurt, mostly with minor cuts and scratches from flying glass.

The very same day, an asteroid came extremely close to Earth, passing between our planet and some of the satellites in HEO. Astronomers say that big meteor and asteroid strikes on Earth are only once-in-a-century occurrences. Over millions of years, though, many such "impact events" have left scars on the land and on the seafloor—from tiny potholes to giant craters.

Space junk is not the only material that can strike Earth from space. Meteors and asteroids also sometimes hit the planet. In 2013 a meteor exploded 14 miles (23 km) in the air above Russia. The shock wave from the explosion damaged buildings in the Russian city of Chelyabinsk.

system to shoot down spy satellites operated by enemy nations. (To date, neither China nor any other nation has actually carried out such a mission.) To test the system, China fired a missile at *Fengyun,* one of its own zombie weather satellites in LEO. Traveling at 18,000 miles (28,970 km) per hour, the missile hit the 1,650-pound (750 kg) zombie at 537 miles (865 km) above Earth. The impact pulverized the satellite, resulting in a cloud of twenty-eight hundred pieces of space junk, including pieces of metal, insulation, and broken solar panels. Two years later, in 2009, the Russian communications satellite *Cosmos 2251* hit the US communications satellite *Iridium 33,* generating more than two thousand additional pieces of space junk. The *Fengyun* and *Cosmos–Iridium* events greatly expanded the amount of junk in orbit.

Meanwhile, space junk creates more space junk. That is, more junk in orbit multiplies the likelihood of more collisions between pieces of junk. In turn, every collision multiplies the overall amount of debris in orbit. Astrophysicist Donald Kessler has been studying space junk since the 1970s. "Even if we add nothing else to orbit, the amount of debris could continue to increase as a result of random collisions between fairly large objects," Kessler said. "You'd generate debris faster than the natural [orbital] decay process could return it [to Earth]." Fraser Cain of the website *Universe Today* describes the situation as "an unstoppable cascade of collisions and chaos that converts the area around Earth into a relentless blender of progressively smaller and smaller high-velocity projectiles. Which would be bad."

The repercussions of space collisions are felt not only in space but also on Earth. Weather forecasts, television broadcasts, Internet communications, airplane and ship navigation, and other human activities all rely on satellites working properly. After the *Cosmos–Iridium* crash in 2009, some customers of Iridium Communications lost cell phone service. Iridium scrambled to put a new satellite online to replace the old one. It had the new satellite up and running just a few days after the crash. Other collisions do even more damage, causing disruptions not only to phone service but also to television broadcasts and air-traffic control operations.

The ESA's *Jules Verne* was an unpiloted cargo spacecraft launched in March 2008. In September 2008, the craft reentered Earth's atmosphere, burning up and breaking apart above the Pacific Ocean. Crew on a NASA aircraft took this photo of *Jules Verne* as it disintegrated.

## ALL FALL DOWN

The higher an orbiting object's altitude, the longer it will remain in orbit before falling to Earth. Objects orbiting more than 621 miles (1,000 km) above Earth will circle the planet for one hundred years or more before falling. Objects at lower altitudes will fall after a few decades or even after just a few years in space—depending on their distance from Earth's surface.

With so much space junk circling Earth and eventually falling, at least one piece of space junk reenters Earth's atmosphere every day. On average, one zombie satellite or rocket stage reenters each week. Most of this material burns up completely when it hits the atmosphere, as a result of the heat generated by friction. But sometimes, sharp flaming pieces of metal have come crashing all the way to Earth's surface. Because oceans cover 71 percent of the planet, most falling space junk lands in the water. But that's not always so.

Skylab, which served as a research station for astronauts in 1973 and early 1974, remained in orbit after the astronauts finished their mission. Beginning in late 1978, the 77-ton (70-metric-ton) space station began a slow but steady fall from orbit, causing alarm on the ground. NASA devised a plan to use a space shuttle to boost Skylab higher into orbit, with the hope that it would remain in orbit for many more years. The US space shuttle program was slated to start in March 1979, but it would take several years to build a shuttle, so the plan wasn't feasible. Meanwhile, Skylab continued to tumble toward Earth. No one at NASA knew what would happen when the research station hit the atmosphere. Would it burn up completely, or would some of the wreckage come crashing to the ground?

NASA engineers still had some control over the craft, so they fired its engines, a move designed to steer it toward the Indian Ocean. As it turned out, the craft fragmented in the heat of reentry. Much of it disintegrated and burned up 10 miles (16 km) above Earth. Some pieces, however, landed in the desert near the small town of Esperance, in the state of Western Australia. Nobody on the ground was harmed. But had the craft not fragmented and burned up, the damage could have been massive. Engineers calculated that the largest sections of Skylab would have hit the ground at speeds of up to 260 miles (418 km) per hour. The debris field might have spread across thousands of miles. Falling and flaming debris might have caused fires, death, and other destruction.

## The Sky Is Falling

When the news that Skylab was falling to Earth reached global citizens in 1979, people were fearful—but many also had a sense of humor about the situation. For example, some Americans wore Skylab T-shirts adorned with large bull's-eyes, as though they were targets for the plummeting spacecraft. After pieces of Skylab landed near Esperance, Australia, the town gave NASA a $400 fine for littering. NASA ignored the fine. Thirty years later, in 2009, a California radio disc jockey named Scott Barley learned that the fine had not been paid. He raised money from his listeners and sent a $400 check to the town of Esperance.

Although Skylab was not designed for reentry, many newer spacecraft are designed to fall back into the atmosphere. For instance, ESA launched the Gravity Field and Steady-State Ocean Circulation Explorer (GOCE) in 2009. The size of a sports utility vehicle, the satellite traveled at a very low orbit, only 140 to 160 miles (225 to 258 km) above Earth. Its mission was to gather data about Earth's atmosphere as well as about ocean currents, polar ice, oil deposits on land, plankton at sea, and climate. The GOCE was designed to reenter the atmosphere and burn up when its fuel ran out. When that happened as expected, in the fall of 2013, the explorer lost altitude at a rate of 2.5 miles (4 km) per day. While most of the GOCE burned up during reentry as planned, some parts of the craft survived the plummet through the atmosphere. On November 11, 600 pounds (272 kg) of space junk from the GOCE crashed into the Atlantic Ocean between Antarctica and South America. No vessels were nearby, and no one was hurt.

About 110 to 165 tons (100 to 150 metric tons) of space junk enter Earth's atmosphere every year, explains Heiner Klinkrad, head of ESA's space debris program. ESA's Holger Krag adds, "Roughly every week you have a re-entry like GOCE." Most of this debris burns up or lands in the ocean, so most people don't know about it. Debris that falls in the ocean simply sinks to the bottom or travels with ocean currents.

## HEADS UP

What are your chances of getting hit by space junk? Mark Matney, a scientist with NASA's Orbital Debris Program, estimates that the chance of any one of Earth's seven billion people being struck is 1 in 3,200. But "the odds that *you* will be hit . . . are 1 in several trillion," said Matney.

A fisherman from Salinópolis, Brazil, found debris from a British spacecraft in a river in 2014. The craft had been launched from French Guiana, in South America, in July 2013.

While the odds of someone being hit by space junk are extremely low, there is nothing to prevent it from happening. Reports of near misses have come from around the world. In 1997 an Oklahoma woman named Lottie Williams was hit on the shoulder by a fist-sized chunk of metal from a US Delta II rocket. (She was unharmed.) This is the only known case of a piece of space debris hitting a human being. More recently,

## The Spacecraft Cemetery

Where do old spaceships go to die? The Spacecraft Cemetery, a portion of the Pacific Ocean where navigation is prohibited, is the final resting place of the Soviet/Russian Mir space station, which arrived there in 2001, and many other defunct craft. If a spacecraft remains fully under human control when it reenters Earth's atmosphere, engineers on the ground can steer it to the Spacecraft Cemetery or another ocean landing spot. Located nearly 2,485 miles (4,000 km) east of Wellington, New Zealand, the Spacecraft Cemetery is 2.5 miles (4 km) deep. Far from shipping lanes, it makes a safe, out-of-the-way dump, where debris rests in a deep trench on the ocean floor. The Mir, at 134 tons (122 metric tons), is the largest craft in the cemetery. Space scientists say that when the ISS is shut down in 2024, it too might be directed to the Spacecraft Cemetery.

in March 2011, a hiker found a 70-pound (32 kg) spherical titanium tank from a Russian rocket in rural Colorado. That month a farmer in the South American nation of Uruguay saw space debris fall from the sky and land nearby. It turned out to be pieces of a US rocket that had been launched into space eight years earlier. One night in February 2015, the American Meteorological Society, an organization devoted to the study of weather, received 195 reports of "fireballs" spotted over the western United States and Canada. NASA later confirmed that the streaks of light were burning pieces of a Chinese rocket that had fragmented upon reentry.

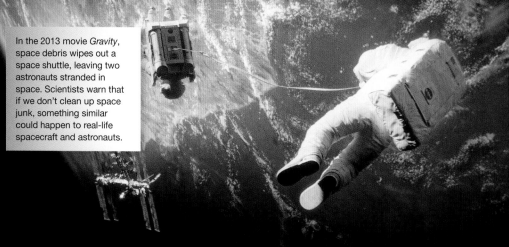

In the 2013 movie *Gravity*, space debris wipes out a space shuttle, leaving two astronauts stranded in space. Scientists warn that if we don't clean up space junk, something similar could happen to real-life spacecraft and astronauts.

∃

# SPACE-TRAFFIC CONTROL

In 1998 there was a close call on the Mir Space Station, and the crew was told to get into the Soyuz [transport capsule] and to prepare in case Mir got hit. . . . Whatever the item was, it travelled at 10 miles [16 km] per second. So at one second it was 10 miles away; two seconds later it was 10 miles the other way. There was no possible way to see it. . . . The shuttle gets hit by some little tiny piece of something on every mission. We just hope it does not happen during an Extravehicular Activity.

—*John M. Grunsfeld, astronomer and astronaut, 2014*

In the award-winning 2013 movie *Gravity,* three astronauts are on a space walk, repairing the Hubble Space Telescope, when debris from a Russian missile strike on a zombie satellite hits their space shuttle. The shuttle is destroyed, and the astronauts on board are killed, as is one of the space walkers. The other two space walkers—the film's heroes (played by Sandra Bullock and George Clooney)—are stranded in space.

Could the *Gravity* story really happen? Yes. While the filmmakers didn't get all the science quite right, the scenario is not far-fetched. Space junk could certainly disable a space vehicle and kill its crew. How can space agencies protect spacecraft and astronauts in orbit? The solutions aren't easy.

The paths that spacecraft take around Earth are not like roadways on the ground. For instance, if you were driving in a car from point A to point B and learned from a radio broadcast or through a smartphone app about a traffic jam or an accident ahead, you might be able to take a side road and avoid the slowdown. In space, avoiding traffic jams isn't always possible. To do their work, many spacecraft need to travel in high-traffic zones, because these zones provide the clearest views of Earth or the best communications channels with the ground. The highest-traffic zone around Earth is LEO. This zone also has the most space junk.

## KEEPING TRACK

The more information that agencies on the ground can gather about space junk, the better they can help spacecraft avoid it. Using radar, telescopes, optical sensors, and data sent back to Earth by orbiting satellites, NASA's Orbital Debris Program, the US Air Force Space Surveillance Network, and the DoD's Space Surveillance Telescope program track pieces

Staff at the ESA's Space Operations Centre in Germany track spacecraft in orbit and try to steer them clear of space debris.

of space junk. Space agencies in other nations also have tracking programs, but they frequently access US tracking data, which is the most accurate and most complete set of data available. Thirteen space agencies, including NASA, the ESA, and others, also coordinate their tracking and space junk research efforts through a group called the Inter-Agency Space Debris Coordination Committee.

## Who Made This Mess?

The nations with the largest space programs are responsible for most of the junk orbiting in space. China is responsible for 40 percent of it—with much of that junk coming from the *Fengyun* missile strike in 2007. The United States is responsible for 27.5 percent of the junk in space, while Russia (and the former Soviet Union) is responsible for 25.5 percent. The remaining 7 percent of the junk comes from space programs in other parts of the world. As more nations develop space programs and as existing programs grow, the percentages will undoubtedly change.

US trackers have identified more than twenty-one thousand pieces of space debris larger than 4 inches (10 cm) across— about the size of a softball. Tracking technology allows for the detection of objects as small as 2 inches (5 cm) across but no smaller. Tracking technology is improving, however. In February 2013, the Canadian Space Agency launched its Near-Earth Object Surveillance Satellite (NEOSSat). Equipped with a telescope, the small satellite is designed to search for large asteroids in the inner solar system as well as for space junk. Because NEOSSat is out in space, it can locate objects farther from Earth than ground-based telescope systems can.

A new program spearheaded by the US aerospace company

Lockheed Martin is called the Space Fence. Slated to go online in 2017, the system will use land-based radar stations and lasers— devices that produce powerful beams of light—to scan LEO for small pieces of space junk, measure the junk, and assess its speed. The Space Fence will be able to track pieces of junk as small as 0.4 inches (1 cm) across, and it will be able to gather data on hundreds of thousands of objects in just a few days. The Space Fence will replace the Air Force's Space Surveillance Network, which has been used since the 1960s. In addition to monitoring space junk, the Space Fence will have a military role. It will help the United States keep tabs on other nations' satellites, especially those carrying out spying missions and other military operations.

## EVASIVE MANEUVERS

Tracking organizations use their data to predict when and where space junk and working satellites or space stations might cross paths. But tracking space junk isn't the same as controlling it. The most that tracking agencies can do is to identify potential collisions and advise operators of spacecraft and space stations to take evasive action.

Before they were grounded permanently in 2011, NASA space shuttles routinely flew upside down and backward to avoid tiny bits of oncoming space debris. The "belly" of the space shuttles—the side that touched the atmosphere first upon reentry—was built to be more resistant to intense heat and pressure than the back of the craft. By flying upside down— turning the belly toward outer space while in orbit—the shuttles could be better protected from debris falling toward Earth. Flying backward placed the windows at the back of the space shuttles, out of the line of fire of any space junk zooming toward a head-on collision with the craft.

In the case of satellites, operators on the ground will fire a craft's rockets, adjusting its altitude or otherwise redirecting its path through space to move it out of the way of oncoming space junk. In September 2014, for example, trackers detected a large object heading straight toward a NASA–NOAA satellite called *Suomi NPP.* Mission controllers repositioned the satellite to prevent a collision. This was the fourth maneuver controllers had made to avoid space junk since *Suomi NPP* was launched in 2011.

With more than eight hundred pieces of debris sharing its orbit, the ISS maneuvers at least once a year to avoid space junk. On October 27, 2014, for example, NASA engineers on the ground directed the space station to leave its normal path to avoid a piece of debris from the 2009 *Cosmos–Iridium* collision. NASA estimated the item to be 3 inches (8 cm) long, about the size of a saltshaker. Three weeks later, NASA directed the ISS to make another evasive move, this time to dodge a 5.5-inch (14 cm) piece of debris from a Chinese satellite launched in 2011.

## NEAR MISSES ON THE ISS

Since the grounding of the space shuttle fleet in 2011, astronauts fly to and from the ISS in transport capsules. Each capsule can hold three astronauts. Normally, six astronauts live on the station at once, which means that two transport capsules are usually docked there. In a few cases, the space junk threat has been enormous.

Astronauts aboard the space shuttle *Discovery* took this photo of the International Space Station in 2011. Flying in a crowded orbit, the ISS faces ongoing threats from space junk.

# Fly Me to the Moon

Have you ever dreamed of flying in space? Someday you might get your wish. The space tourism industry kicked off in April 2001, when Russia's space agency sent US businessman Dennis Tito to the ISS for a one-week stay with the astronauts there. Tito paid $20 million for the trip. Since then, a handful of other tourists have visited the ISS, but space tourism remains a rare and extremely expensive undertaking.

Several companies, including Virgin Galactic, want to make space tourism more common and more affordable. Virgin Galactic has built a facility called Spaceport America in the New Mexico desert. From there it hopes to take hundreds of paying passengers on spaceflights lasting two and a half hours. Out in space, passengers will experience adventure, an amazing view, and weightlessness, the sensation of being free from the strong pull of Earth's gravity. As of early 2015, about eight hundred people had made down payments toward future flights with Virgin Galactic. Among them are some famous names: physicist Stephen Hawking, musicians Justin Bieber and Katy Perry, and actor Tom Hanks.

Virgin Galactic suffered a setback when one of its spaceships crashed in a test flight in October 2014. In addition, many experts expect the FAA to put strict regulations on space tourism in the United States, further delaying affordable space travel. Finally, threats from space junk might also limit future space tourism, along with other kinds of space travel.

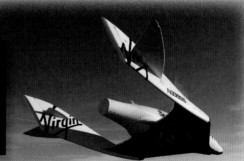

Virgin Galactic's *SpaceShipTwo (right)* crashed during a test flight in October 2014. One pilot was killed in the crash. The company is building new spaceships and continuing with plans to take tourists into space.

## DRAGONS in Space

By 2016 the ISS will carry a new sensor to measure space debris that is too small to be detected by trackers on the ground. NASA crew will mount this sensor, called the Debris Resistive/Acoustic Grid Orbital Navy Sensor (DRAGONS), on the outside of the shuttle. DRAGONS will measure the impact of microscopic debris hitting the ISS to determine its size, speed, and direction of travel. The sensor will be able to analyze space junk as small as 50 microns—about the width of a human hair. It will not help the ISS to avoid the debris but, instead, will gather data that will help scientists better understand the behavior of microscopic debris particles.

Astronauts on the ISS have had to temporarily suspend their work on the space station and move into the transport capsules—just in case they needed to make a quick return to Earth. For the ISS, any piece of junk closer than 2.8 miles (4.5 km) is considered a serious threat.

In November 2014, the ISS experienced its nearest near miss ever, when a chunk of *Cosmos 2251* (the Russian zombie involved in the big 2009 collision) sailed into its path. The junk was predicted to pass the ISS at a distance of just 2.5 miles (4 km)—far too close for comfort. An ESA cargo vehicle had just delivered a load of supplies to the space station and was still docked there. Six hours before the piece of *Cosmos* junk was supposed to reach the ISS, controllers in France fired the cargo vehicle's thrusters. The moving cargo vehicle acted like a tugboat—pushing the ISS for 0.6 miles (1 km)—safely out of the path of the speeding space junk.

# The Flying Russian

Like other people, astronauts have to take out the trash. When the ISS gets too crowded with used equipment and other garbage, astronauts load it into empty cargo vehicles and send them back into Earth's atmosphere to burn up on reentry.

In 2006 Russian astronauts on the ISS had a little fun with trash disposal. They stuffed an old space suit *(right)* with old clothes and other garbage, named it Ivan Ivanovich (a common Russian name), and launched it back to Earth. They equipped it with a radio transmitter and as Ivan circled Earth, astronauts on the ISS tracked him via radio. The phony astronaut burned up on reentry after orbiting Earth for 216 days.

The stunt seemed funny in 2006, but that was before the *Fengyun* and *Cosmos–Iridium* events, which blasted space junk numbers sky-high. Astronauts in the 2010s are aware of the growing danger of space junk and would be unlikely to deliberately release even more junk into space.

# BETTER BUMPERS

Thus far, tracking systems can help spacecraft avoid large pieces of debris but not tiny fragments that are smaller than a marble. Inevitably, some of these small pieces are bound to strike a craft. For protection, many spacecraft are equipped with metallic plates called Whipple shields or Whipple bumpers (named for US astronomer Fred Whipple, who invented the devices in the 1940s). About two hundred Whipple shields protect the walls of the ISS.

The multilayer shields have aluminum on the outside. Inner layers consist of Nextel, a strong ceramic fabric, and Kevlar, the material used to make bulletproof vests. When a speeding piece of debris hits a Whipple shield, it might dent or puncture the outer, aluminum layer of the shield. If it punctures the aluminum, the inner fabric layers provide a backup to slow and stop the object. Often, when an object strikes a Whipple shield, the tremendous force of the impact causes the object

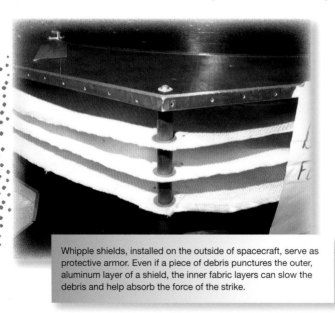

Whipple shields, installed on the outside of spacecraft, serve as protective armor. Even if a piece of debris punctures the outer, aluminum layer of a shield, the inner fabric layers can slow the debris and help absorb the force of the strike.

to disintegrate into a cloud of even tinier pieces of debris. This disintegration spreads the force of the impact over a larger area, minimizing its damage to the Whipple shield and to the spacecraft.

Whipple shields can protect spacecraft from tiny debris particles, up to about 0.1 inches (3 millimeters) across. Teams from NASA's Orbital Debris Program and the US Department of Defense are working to develop shields that can protect spacecraft against even larger pieces of space junk.

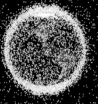

This illustration from NASA shows that high Earth orbit is crowded with spacecraft, although it's not as crowded as low Earth orbit. Many zombies orbit in the Geostationary Graveyard, above geostationary orbit in HEO.

# 4

# TAKING OUT THE TRASH

If we don't do anything, space will soon become inaccessible because of the large amount of debris and the high risk of collision.

—Claude Nicollier, Swiss astronaut and technical adviser for the debris cleanup project CleanSpace One, 2012

In 1959 the United Nations (UN), an international peacekeeping and humanitarian organization, created the Committee on the Peaceful Uses of Outer Space (COPUOS). Over the years, the committee has drafted international guidelines and policies regarding space exploration and research. In 2008 the committee turned its attention to space junk. It adopted a set of "Space Debris Mitigation Guidelines." The guidelines are designed to limit the amount of debris created by spacecraft during launch, orbiting, and reentry; to limit the potential for collisions in orbit; and to limit the amount of time spacecraft can remain in orbit after their operations are completed. For instance, Guideline 6 advises, "Spacecraft . . . that have terminated their operational phases in orbits that pass through the LEO region should be removed from orbit in a controlled fashion. If this is not possible, they should be disposed of in orbits that avoid their long-term presence in the LEO region."

Seventy-seven nations send representatives to COPUOS, and satellite operators in these nations are asked to voluntarily sign on to the migration guidelines. So the guidelines are not laws, and nations cannot be punished for ignoring them. Voluntary guidelines might not be enough, however. The Inter-Agency Space Debris Coordination Committee (IADC) is an international council of thirteen space agencies from around the world, formed to improve communications between countries with spacecraft in orbit. In 2013 the IADC announced that if additional measures were not taken, debris in LEO would increase greatly over the next century, and collisions would skyrocket as well.

## PULLED IN BY GRAVITY

In addition to thrilling audiences, the 2013 movie *Gravity* focused attention on the damage that space junk can do. It led to a multitude of media reports on the dangers of space junk and was the focus of *Space Traffic Management: How to Prevent a Real Life "Gravity,"* a May 2014 hearing among US congressional representatives. At the hearing, space scientists and engineers warned government officials that space travel and satellite operation would become more and more dangerous because of increasing amounts of space junk. The experts said that new legislation, government oversight, and safety practices needed to limit space debris and to protect spacecraft. They urged Congress to create a new federal agency to supervise all US satellites, a job that's currently shared by NASA, NOAA, DoD, FAA, and the FCC.

While the hearing focused attention on the problem of space debris, it did not lead immediately to concrete action. At a November 2014 conference organized by the Center for Orbital Debris Education and Research at the University of Maryland, NASA's Thomas Cremins said that more work needed to be done. "This past year, we've spent a lot of time thinking about [space junk] remediation [remedies]," said Cremins. But he noted that NASA did "not have an active debris remediation program."

## ZERO POPULATION GROWTH

Although concrete plans are limited, scientists, engineers, and satellite operators around the world have many ideas about how to reduce or remove space junk. One simple idea is to quit putting as much junk into space in the first place. New satellites will continue to go into orbit, but some experts advocate a requirement that all new satellites be designed to return to Earth after their missions are complete. That is, they would no longer be allowed to drift in space for years and even decades. They would have to return to Earth either through their own power or through retrieval by a robotic space vehicle.

In addition, some scientists support a policy of "one-up, one-down." They argue that if a government or business launches a new satellite, it should be required to bring down another, nonoperational satellite from the same orbit. But experts say that this approach would not solve the problem. They say that even if no new satellites were sent to LEO, the number of objects 4 inches (10 cm) and larger would continue to increase, because the debris that is already in space would continue to smash into other objects, creating more debris.

## Rolling Thunder

In April 2014, a group of organizations including the US Air Force and NASA destroyed a full-scaled mock satellite called *DebriSat* in a ground test chamber in Tennessee. It took two years to design and build the mock satellite—and just seconds to destroy it.

Testers blasted the satellite with a 1.2-pound (544-gram) soup-can-sized projectile at more than 15,210 miles (24,478 km) per hour. The strike took place inside a foam-lined chamber, designed to catch the flying debris. The sound of the impact "was like rolling thunder," said Jer-Chyi Liou, NASA's chief scientist for orbital debris. The impact created eighty-five thousand fragments of different shapes and sizes. A corps of student volunteers counted, sorted, and analyzed the fragments.

The test will help engineers better understand collisions in space and how space debris travels after a crash. By learning how space junk behaves, scientists can figure out better ways to protect spacecraft from space junk and better ways to clean up the junk.

# WAKE THE DEAD

While some defunct spacecraft rest permanently in the Spacecraft Cemetery in the Pacific Ocean, other defunct craft orbit permanently in the Geostationary Graveyard, a zone between 155 and 186 miles (250 and 300 km) above geostationary orbit. Operators on Earth deliberately direct some satellites to this graveyard, firing their rockets one last time to get them there before taking them off-line. The goal is to move zombies far away from operational satellites to minimize crashes. But even the Geostationary Graveyard is getting

At the Massachusetts Institute of Technology, Alvar Saenz-Otero and his team of aerospace scientists are building robots that can dock with zombie satellites for repair or refueling missions.

crowded. And zombies will eventually decay out of the graveyard and might collide with operational spacecraft or even come crashing back to Earth.

It's not unusual for operational satellites to malfunction or break while in orbit. However, repairing a damaged satellite can be extremely expensive. It's more economical for a satellite operator to let a broken satellite drift and to launch a new, functional satellite to take its place. But with so many zombies in orbit, scientists are rethinking this approach. Both space agencies and private companies are developing systems for refueling or repairing zombies. For example, NASA tested one refueling system in 2014. In a trial run, a robotic vehicle successfully transferred a load of nitrogen tetroxide, a propellant commonly used to power satellites, into a dummy satellite.

Another machine in the testing phase, NASA's Visual Inspection Poseable Invertebrate Robot (VIPIR), is also designed to repower zombie satellites. It can carry out tasks such as replenishing cryogen, another satellite fuel, and installing new solar panels on satellites to revive dead or dying ones. To determine what task to perform, VIPIR eyeballs the situation first. Using a tiny camera on a tube, VIPIR sends pictures back to NASA mission control, waits for a problem assessment, and then carries out commands to fix the problem.

The Department of Defense needs to keep its spy satellites in working order to protect national security. Through a program called Phoenix, the DoD hopes to not only repair zombie satellites in space but to even assemble new ones in orbit. The plan is to send robots to repair disabled satellites, using replacement parts that the robots have salvaged from other damaged, orbiting satellites.

## TRICKY BUSINESS

Refueling and repairing zombies won't be easy, however. The robots that will carry out such missions will need to link up with satellites traveling through space at thousands of miles per hour. If missions aren't executed with precision, the robots could crash into the zombies, creating more space junk.

What's more, zombie satellites, with no human controllers keeping them on course, tend to tumble through space as they travel. Before a refueling or repair craft can dock, or link, with a tumbling zombie, scientists have to figure out the direction, rate, and angle of the tumble and then get the two vehicles in sync. This job requires advanced mathematics. At the Massachusetts Institute of Technology (MIT), a scientific team led by Alvar Saenz-Otero, director of MIT's AeroAstro Space Systems Lab, has crunched the numbers and developed an algorithm, or mathematical formula, to guide engineers as they sync up crafts in space. Successfully tested on a small satellite at the ISS, the algorithm will help unmanned robotic satellites dock with zombies, get on board, reboot them, and put them back to work in the right orbit.

Even after a successful docking, however, zombies will have to be handled gingerly. Many zombies contain unspent fuel or batteries that still carry an electrical charge. If bumped or jarred with too much force, a zombie could explode, taking the cleanup robot with it and creating yet more space junk.

# Stories of Space Junk

The space junk phenomenon has inspired writers, filmmakers, and other artists. Science fiction author Arthur C. Clarke wrote about space junk in his 1979 novel *The Fountains of Paradise*. Set in the twenty-second century, the book features a program called Operation Cleanup, with big spaceships that use lasers to zap debris out of orbit. In the Japanese anime TV series *Planetes* (2003–2004), which takes place in the year 2075, humans work as space debris collectors, jetting around space cleaning up. In the 2008 animated film *Wall-E,* set in 2805, space junk surrounding Earth is so thick that travelers have to dodge it to get out of orbit.

In the Japanese TV series *Planetes*, set in the year 2075, human janitors clean up space junk piece by piece.

*Gravity* (2013) gives the most realistic picture of space junk, painting a scenario that could possibly happen to twenty-first-century astronauts. The screenwriters used the real-life Chinese missile strike on *Fengyun* as the basis for their tale. In the movie, the space debris that strikes the astronauts and their shuttle is generated by a fictional Russian missile strike on a defunct satellite.

## HOUSE CLEANING

Some pieces of space junk are just that—junk. These objects can't be repaired or reused. The best option is to bring them back to Earth's atmosphere, where they will burn up on reentry. Space agencies and private businesses around the world are working on several programs to make this a reality.

In August 2014, the Russian space agency, Roscocosmos, budgeted about $297 million to design and build a spaceship to clean up geostationary orbit. Called the Liquidator, the craft will either push zombie satellites and rocket stages into the

Geostationary Graveyard or pull them into the atmosphere for reentry, where they will burn up or possibly fall into the Spacecraft Cemetery in the Pacific. The plan is for twice-yearly missions for ten years. The project is expected to remove twenty large pieces of space junk per year and to eventually expand to bring in more.

The ESA has begun several test programs designed to retrieve zombie satellites from geostationary orbit. One of these is CubeSail, based at the Surrey Space Centre at the University of Surrey in Britain. The program aims to bring down space debris using devices called solar sails, made of Mylar, a type of plastic film. Small satellites will carry the furled-up sails into space. Out in space, the sails will unfurl to their full size— as big as barns. Large numbers of photons, or tiny particles of sunlight, will hit the sails, creating enough pressure to push them through space and back toward Earth. At the same time, the sails will retrieve space junk and carry it with them back into Earth's orbit.

The Japan Aerospace Exploration Agency (JAXA) is developing a device called an electrodynamic tether, which will work sort of like a fishing net sweeping through LEO. (In fact, JAXA worked with fishing equipment engineers to design the device.) The tether is a 2,300-foot (700 m) net made of stainless steel and aluminum that will be carried into orbit on a spacecraft. Sensors on the net will pick up glimmers of light reflecting off metal space debris. The net will generate electricity as it swings through Earth's magnetic field, a region of magnetism that surrounds the planet. (Magnetism is a force created by an electrical charge.) The electricity will attract debris to the net. Once the net has snagged enough junk, it will travel back to the atmosphere and drop the junk for reentry.

Star, Inc., a South Carolina company, is developing a device called an ElectroDynamic Debris Eliminator (EDDE). The device will travel into space with an LEO satellite. It will be folded up for travel into a package measuring just 4 cubic feet (0.12 cu. m). In space it will unfold to its full size of 1 mile (1.6 km) in length. EDDE consists of a long piece of electricity-conducting material, solar arrays that generate electrical current, and lightweight nets. Earth's magnetism will interact with EDDE's electric current to move the craft through space. The nets will capture space junk and tow it back to the atmosphere. Star says that in seven years, twelve EDDEs could remove nearly twenty-five hundred pieces of small space junk (weighing less than 4.4 pounds [2 kg] each) from LEO. The small items would burn up upon reentry.

Raytheon BBN Technologies in Virginia and engineers at the University of Michigan are working on a system called Space Debris Elimination (SpaDE). The plan involves using balloons or airplanes traveling high in the atmosphere. They will fire strong pulses of atmospheric gases at pieces of space debris. The pulses will create extra drag on the debris, pulling it back toward Earth. One plus of this project is that it will operate in the atmosphere rather than in space, without sending into orbit any new spacecraft that could eventually become space debris.

Two engineers at Texas A&M University, Daniele Mortari and Jonathan Missel, have high hopes for their TAMU Sweeper. This is a cube-shaped satellite with two long, expanding arms. At the end of each arm is a device that can snag debris and fling it toward Earth's atmosphere. The flinging motion will also give the sweeper a push forward, moving it toward the next piece of space junk. This system will save on fuel because it will propel itself through space.

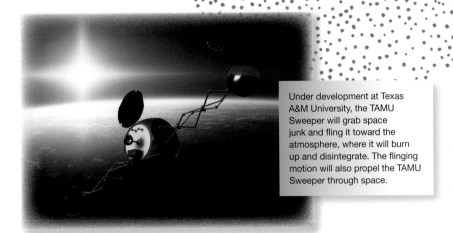

Under development at Texas A&M University, the TAMU Sweeper will grab space junk and fling it toward the atmosphere, where it will burn up and disintegrate. The flinging motion will also propel the TAMU Sweeper through space.

The list of additional ideas for cleaning up space goes on and on. For instance, the ESA is working on a machine called the e.DeOrbit. It will be launched into orbit on a Vega rocket and will catch up with targeted space junk in well-traveled orbital paths in LEO. The device will snag the junk with nets, harpoons, or robotic tentacles and then haul it back to the atmosphere. A Swiss company called Swiss Space Systems has built a device called CleanSpace One. It will use soft tentacle-like arms to reach out and capture small zombie satellites and carry them back to the atmosphere. Swiss Space Systems plans to send CleanSpace One into orbit with the *SOAR* space plane in 2018. Other ideas for cleaning up space junk involve shooting it down with giant lasers.

## THE TIME HAS COME

Building cleanup vehicles and sending them into orbit will cost nations and satellite operators billions of dollars. But consider that a typical weather satellite costs $290 million to build and between $10 million and $400 million to launch into space. A satellite operator that has invested this much money does not want to see its machine wiped out in an instant by space junk. So it makes economic sense to invest money in space

## Clarke's Cleanup

"The old orbital forts were superbly equipped for [cleaning up space junk]. Their radars . . . could easily pinpoint the debris of the early space age. Then their lasers vaporized the smaller satellites, while the larger ones were nudged into higher and harmless orbits.

"Some, of historic interest, were recovered and brought back to Earth. During this operation there were quite a few surprises—for example, three Chinese astronauts who had perished on some secret mission, and several reconnaissance satellites constructed from such an ingenious mix of components that it was quite impossible to discover what country had launched them. Not, of course, that it now mattered a great deal, since they were at least a hundred years old."

—*Arthur C. Clarke,*
The Fountains of Paradise,
*a fictional description of space junk cleanup, 1979*

cleanup—especially if agencies and businesses from several nations get together to share the cost.

It's not only economically sound to clean up space. Satellites are vital to our modern way of life. We need them for cell phone and Internet communications. Many people check the weather forecast for their town or region every day. Weather forecasts are created from images and data gathered by satellites. For safe travel, airplanes, ships, and passenger vehicles all rely on GPS navigation systems, which in turn rely on GPS satellites. Military forces—which are tasked with protecting the safety of citizens—depend on spy satellites to gather accurate information about military threats. And future explorations of the solar system and the space beyond it depend on our ability to safely travel to and from Planet Earth. Taking control of the space around Earth and making it safe for travel and technology is one of the most important tasks for humans in the twenty-first century.

Donald Kessler is called the Father of Space Junk because he was one of the first scientists to sound the alarm about the problem. In 1978 Kessler first described how collisions would lead to more space junk and more collisions, creating an ever-growing mass of junk in space—a phenomenon called the Kessler syndrome. More than thirty-five years later, Kessler's predictions are starting to come true. As senior NASA scientist Jack Bacon explains, "The Kessler syndrome is in effect. We're in a runaway environment, and we won't be able to use space in the future if we don't start dealing with this now."

# Timeline

**1957:** The Space Age begins on October 4 when the Soviet Union launches *Sputnik 1*, the world's first human-made satellite, into orbit.

**1959:** *Luna 2*, a Soviet spacecraft, crash-lands on the moon, becoming the moon's first piece of space junk.

**1961:** *Transit 4A*, a US rocket, explodes in space after successfully launching a military satellite. Debris from the explosion becomes the first space junk in orbit.

**1978:** US astrophysicist Donald Kessler describes how space junk creates more space junk. He explains that when objects collide in space, they shatter into hundreds or thousands of fragments and that each fragment has the potential to hit other objects, in turn creating more space junk.

Skylab, a nonoperational US research station for astronauts, begins to fall out of orbit. It reaches Earth's atmosphere in July 1979. Much of the craft burns up on reentry, but some pieces land in the desert near Esperance, Australia.

**1997:** Oklahoman Lottie Williams is hit on the shoulder by a small piece of metal from a US Delta II rocket. She is the only person known to have been hit by space junk.

**2001:** The Soviet/Russian space station Mir ends its operations. The Russian space agency guides Mir back to Earth's atmosphere. Some of it burns up on reentry, and the remainder falls into the Spacecraft Cemetery in the Pacific Ocean.

**2003:** The US space shuttle *Columbia* explodes during reentry. All seven crewmembers die in the explosion, and debris from the craft lands in eastern Texas and western Louisiana.

**2006:** Russian astronauts on the International Space Station release a space suit filled with trash into orbit. Nicknamed Ivan Ivanovich, the space suit orbits Earth for 216 days before burning up on reentry.

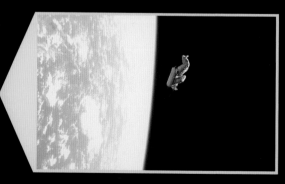

**2007:** The Chinese government fires a missile at *Fengyun,* a Chinese zombie weather satellite, to test a system for shooting down enemy spy satellites. Upon impact, *Fengyun* breaks apart into twenty-eight hundred pieces of space junk.

**2009:** The zombie Russian communications satellite *Cosmos 2251* crashes into the US communications satellite *Iridium 33.* Upon impact, the satellites shatter into more than twenty-one hundred pieces of space junk.

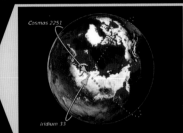

**2012:** The European Space Agency loses contact with *Envisat,* a research satellite launched in 2002. *Envisat* becomes the largest zombie satellite in low Earth orbit.

**2013:** A meteor explodes in the air above the Russian city of Chelyabinsk. The shock wave from the explosion damages buildings and injures more than one thousand people. In the Hollywood movie *Gravity,* space junk destroys a space shuttle and leaves two astronauts stranded in space. The movie helps bring attention to the space junk problem.

**2014:** The International Space Station makes several maneuvers to avoid pieces of debris created by the 2009 *Cosmos–Iridium* crash. The US National Aeronautics and Space Administration tests its Visual Inspection Poseable Invertebrate Robot, a system for repairing and repowering zombie satellites in space. In a test chamber in Tennessee, the US Air Force and NASA destroy *DebriSat,* a mock satellite, to learn more about how debris travels after a crash in space.

**2015:** A US Air Force weather satellite explodes in space after its power system fails. The explosion creates more than one hundred trackable pieces of space junk and more than fifty thousand pieces of junk too small to track.

# Source Notes

6 "Kessler Syndrome," *Space Safety Magazine,* accessed April 1, 2015, http://www.spacesafetymagazine.com/space-debris/kessler-syndrome/.

10 "Removing Space Debris: TAMU Sweeper with Sling-Sat," YouTube, 8:03, posted by "Jonathan Missel Media," July 17, 2012, https://www.youtube.com/watch?v=Aoow-t7qu7k.

11 Evan I. Schwartz, "The Looming Space Junk Crisis: It's Time to Take Out the Trash," *Wired,* May 24, 2010, http://www.wired.com/2010/05/ff_space_junk/all/.

20 Natalie Wolchover, "What Are the Odds You'll Get Struck by a Falling Satellite?," *LiveScience,* September 21, 2011, http://www.livescience.com/33511-falling-nasa-satellite-uars-risk.html.

24 Fraser Cain, "How Can We Clean Up That Space Junk?" *Universe Today,* August 14, 2014, http://www.universetoday.com/113884/how-can-we-clean-up-that-space-junk/.

27 Liz Fuller-Wright, "Splashdown! Falling GOCE Satellite Lands in the Atlantic," *Christian Science Monitor,* November 11, 2013, http://www.csmonitor.com/Science/2013/1111/Splashdown!-Falling-GOCE-satellite-lands-in-the-Atlantic.

27 Wolchover, "What Are the Odds."

30 Roger D. Launius and David H. DeVorkin, eds., *Hubble's Legacy: Reflections by Those Who Dreamed It, Built It, and Observed the Universe with It* (Washington, DC: Smithsonian Institution Scholarly Press, 2014), 69.

40 "How To Clean Up Space Junk," YouTube video, 6:08, posted by "Veritasium," November 26, 2012, https://www.youtube.com/watch?v=6wr_Zw1uGY8.

41 "Space Debris Mitigation Guidelines of the Committee on the Peaceful Use of Outer Space," United Nations Office for Outer Space Affairs, accessed April 1, 2015, http://www.iadc-online.org/References/Docu/Space_Debris_Mitigation_Guidelines_COPUOS.pdf.

42 Jeff Foust, "Cleaning Up Space Junk," *Space Review,* December 15, 2014, http://www.thespacereview.com/article/2663/1.

43 Leonard David, "Mock Satellite Destroyed to Study Space Junk Collisions," Space.com, October 28, 2014, http://www.space.com/27555-debrisat-space-junk-collisions.html.

50 Arthur C. Clarke, *The Fountains of Paradise* (New York: Harcourt Brace Jovanovich, 1979), page 175.

51 Schwartz, "Looming Space Junk Crisis."

# Glossary

**altitude:** the height of an object above Earth's surface

**artificial satellite:** a human-made vehicle designed to orbit Earth or another body in space. People use artificial satellites to gather data about weather and other phenomena on Earth, to send and receive communication signals, to photograph regions of Earth, and to assist with navigation, among other jobs.

**asteroid:** a small rocky or metallic object orbiting the sun. Asteroids sometimes crash into spacecraft and sometimes hit Earth's atmosphere.

**atmosphere:** a layer of gases surrounding a planet or another body in space. Earth's atmosphere has five layers: (from bottom to top) the troposphere, stratosphere, mesosphere, thermosphere, and exosphere. Some satellites travel in the top two layers.

**big-sky theory:** the idea, accepted in the early days of space exploration and later shown to be inaccurate, that the space around Earth was so large that objects orbiting there were unlikely to collide with one another

**drag:** a force that slows an object moving through liquid or gas, such as a satellite moving through the atmosphere

**dwell time:** the amount of time a satellite remains over a certain region of Earth

**elliptical orbit:** an oval-shaped path traveled by a satellite. Artificial satellites that travel in elliptical orbits allow for extended views of far northern or far southern parts of Earth.

**extravehicular activity (EVA):** repairs, tests, and other activities that astronauts carry out outside of space vehicles. Another name for an EVA is a space walk.

**friction:** the rubbing of one thing against another. Friction naturally creates heat and also slows down moving objects.

**Geostationary Graveyard:** an area in space above geostationary orbit. Satellite operators often send zombie satellites to the Geostationary Graveyard, where they are left to drift.

**geostationary orbit:** an orbit that matches the speed of Earth as it spins on its axis, a geometric line running through the center of the planet. Objects in geostationary orbit stay over one point on the globe at all times.

gravity: a naturally occurring force that pulls objects in space toward one another. Earth orbits the sun and spacecraft orbit Earth because of the pull of gravity.

high Earth orbit: any orbit higher than 22,233 miles (35,780 km) above Earth's surface

International Space Station (ISS): a large satellite built in space by more than fifteen nations. The ISS serves as a residence for astronauts, who carry out research projects there.

Kessler syndrome: the idea, first proposed by US astrophysicist Donald Kessler in the 1970s, that space junk creates more space junk. Kessler explained that when objects collide in space, they shatter into hundreds or thousands of fragments. Each of these fragments has the potential to hit other objects, in turn creating more space junk.

lasers: devices that produce powerful beams of light. Among many other uses, laser beams can scan Earth's orbit for space junk. Some engineers propose using them to knock space junk into reentry.

low Earth orbit: an orbit at 112 to 1,242 miles (180 to 2,000 km) above Earth's surface

magnetism: a force created by an electrical charge. Scientists propose using Earth's magnetism to propel space cleanup vehicles and to collect and move space junk.

meteor: a rocky or metallic object flying through space. Meteors sometimes crash into spacecraft and sometimes hit Earth's atmosphere.

mid-Earth orbit: an orbit at 1,243 to 22,233 miles (2,000 to 35,780 km) above Earth

National Aeronautics and Space Administration (NASA): A US government agency that manages the nation's nonmilitary space program and conducts research on aircraft flight. NASA operates some satellites and also space-debris tracking programs.

orbit: to travel around another object. For example, the moon orbits Earth, and planets orbit the sun. The path an object travels in space around another object is also called its orbit.

orbital decay: the process by which objects in orbit lose altitude, move out of their original orbit, and are pulled toward Earth

radar: a system that emits and receives radio waves. Engineers use radar to track both fixed and moving objects on the ground and in space.

**reentry:** moving through Earth's atmosphere after travel in space. Many objects disintegrate or burn up upon reentry. Others crash into the ocean or occasionally onto land.

**satellite:** a natural or human-made object that orbits another object in space

**solar power:** energy derived from the sun's rays. Many space vehicles are fueled by solar power.

**Spacecraft Cemetery:** a region in the South Pacific Ocean that serves as the final resting place for many defunct spacecraft. If humans maintain control over a defunct spacecraft, they might steer it toward the Spacecraft Cemetery as it falls from orbit.

**space junk:** sometimes referred to as space debris, any human-made object traveling through space (or sitting on the moon or a planet) that is not controlled by people on Earth

**weightlessness:** freedom from the pull of gravity. Astronauts experience weightlessness when they leave Earth's atmosphere.

**Whipple shield:** a plate made of layers of aluminum and strong fabric, used to protect the outside of spacecraft from tiny pieces of space debris

**zombie satellite:** a satellite that is out of operation and no longer in communication with controllers on Earth

# Selected Bibliography

Amos, Jonathan. "European Space Agency's GOCE Satellite Falls to Earth." *BBC News*, November 11, 2013. http://www.bbc.com/news /science-environment-24894611.

Cain, Fraser. "How Can We Clean Up That Space Junk?" *Universe Today*, August 14, 2014. http://www.universetoday.com/113884/how-can -we-clean-up-that-space-junk/.

———. "How Many Satellites Are in Space?" *Universe Today*, October 24, 2013. http://www.universetoday.com/42198/how-many -satellites-in-space/.

Chow, Denise. "Clean Up Space Junk or Risk 'Gravity'-Type Disaster, Experts Say." *CBS News*, May 12, 2014. http://www.cbsnews.com /news/clean-up-space-junk-or-risk-gravity-type-disaster-experts-say/.

Clark, Stuart. "Space Junk: Hunting Zombies in Outer Space." *New Scientist*, September 15, 2010. http://www.newscientist.com /article/mg20727772.300-space-junk-hunting-zombies-in-outer -space.html#.VOurkMazh3N.

Klinkrad, Heiner. *Space Debris: Models and Risk Analysis.* Berlin: Springer, 2014.

La Vone, Michelle. "Kessler Syndrome." *Space Safety Magazine.* Accessed February 23, 2015. http://www.spacesafetymagazine .com/space-debris/kessler-syndrome/.

McKinnon, Mika. "A History of Garbage in Space." Space.io9, May 7, 2014. http://space.io9.com/a-history-of-garbage-in -space-1572783046.

NASA. "Orbital Debris Research at NASA." Orbital Debris Program Office. Last modified October 2, 2012. http://orbitaldebris.jsc.nasa.gov.

———. "Three Classes of Orbit." Earth Observatory. Accessed February 23, 2015. http://earthobservatory.nasa.gov/Features /OrbitsCatalog/page2.php.

O'Neill, Ian. "Space Station Sacrifices Progress Module to Dump Trash into Pacific." *Universe Today*, April 9, 2008. http://www .universetoday.com/13545/space-station-sacrifices-progress -module-to-dump-trash-into-pacific/.

Quenqua, Douglas. "Watch out for Falling Space Junk and Asteroids." *New York Times*, November 11, 2013.

Redd, Nola Taylor. "Space Junk: Tracking and Removing Orbital Debris." Space.com, March 8, 2013. http://www.space.com/16518-space -junk.html.

Schwartz, Evan I. "The Looming Space Junk Crisis: It's Time to Take Out the Trash." *Wired,* May 24, 2010. http://www.wired.com/2010/05 /ff_space_junk/.

# Further Information

## Books

Aguilar, David A. *Space Encyclopedia: A Tour of Our Solar System and Beyond.* Washington, DC: National Geographic Kids, 2013.

Bizony, Piers. *New Space Frontiers: Venturing into Earth Orbit and Beyond.* Minneapolis: Zenith, 2014.

Goodman, Susan E. *How Do You Burp in Space? And Other Tips Every Space Tourist Needs to Know.* New York: Bloomsbury, 2013.

Hadfield, Chris. *You Are Here: Around the World in Ninety-Two Minutes.* New York: Little, Brown, 2014.

Koppes, Steven. *Killer Rocks from Outer Space: Asteroids, Comets, and Meteorites.* Minneapolis: Twenty-First Century Books, 2004.

McMahon, Peter. *Space Tourism.* Toronto: Kids Can Press, 2011.

Miller, Ron. *Curiosity's Mission on Mars: Exploring the Red Planet.* Minneapolis: Twenty-First Century Books, 2014.

———. *Robot Explorers.* Minneapolis: Twenty-First Century Books, 2008.

———. *Satellites.* Minneapolis: Twenty-First Century Books, 2008.

———. *Space Exploration.* Minneapolis: Twenty-First Century Books, 2008.

Moltz, James Clay. *Crowded Orbits: Conflict and Cooperation in Space.* New York: Columbia University Press, 2014.

Silverman, Buffy. *Exploring Dangers in Space: Asteroids, Space Junk, and More.* Minneapolis: Lerner Publications, 2012.

Tyson, Neil deGrasse. *Space Chronicles: Facing the Ultimate Frontier.* Edited by Avis Lang. New York: W. W. Norton, 2014.

## Videos

"From Above: Astronaut Photography with Don Pettit." YouTube video, 4:24. Posted by "SmugMug Films," December 10, 2014. https://www.youtube.com/watch?v=rwt3kMivZk4.
In this short film, astronauts describe photographing Earth from space and show their awe-inspiring images.

*Gravity.* DVD. Burbank, CA: Warner Brothers, 2013.
Starring Sandra Bullock and George Clooney, the Hollywood blockbuster tells the story of two astronauts who struggle to survive after space junk wipes out their space shuttle and its crew. The film won Academy Awards for cinematography, directing, editing, sound editing and mixing, visual effects, and more.

"How to Clean Up Space Junk." YouTube video, 6:08. Posted by
   "Veritasium," November 26, 2012. https://www.youtube.com
   /watch?v=6wr_Zw1uGY8.
   This video explains the space junk problem and introduces
   CleanSpace One, a Swiss program designed to clean up some
   of the debris.
*Space Junk 3D*. DVD. Minneapolis: Melrae Pictures, 2013.
   This award-winning movie explores the space junk threat using
   dramatic 3-D images.

## Websites

ESA Kids
   http://www.esa.int/esaKIDSen/index.html
   This kid-friendly website from the European Space Agency offers
   information on the universe, life in space, space technology, and
   planet Earth. The site includes a section called "Fishing for
   Space Junk."

International Space Station
   http://www.nasa.gov/mission_pages/station/main/
   This website from NASA introduces visitors to the International
   Space Station, with material on ISS astronauts, research projects,
   life aboard the station, and more.

Space Junk Clean Up: Seven Wild Ways to Destroy Orbital Debris
   http://www.space.com/24895-space-junk-wild-clean-up-concepts
   .html
   The space and astronomy website Space.com presents an
   overview of seven proposed space cleanup projects, including the
   TAMU Sweeper and CleanSpace One.

Space Junk Explained: How Orbital Debris Threatens Future of
   Spaceflight
   http://www.space.com/23039-space-junk-explained-orbital-debris
   -infographic.html
   Here Space.com uses striking graphic images to explain the space
   junk problem and possible solutions. Space.com is a great source
   for up-to-date information on space debris and related issues.

# Index

63

# Photo Acknowledgments

The images in this book are used with the permission of: NASA Orbital Debris Program Office, pp. 2–3, 10, 40; NASA/JPL, p. 6; © Iridium Communications Inc., p. 7; US Navy, p. 9; NASA/Goddard Space Flight Center/United Launch Alliance, p. 13; © Laura Westlund/Independent Picture Service, pp. 16, 18; © European Space Agency/Denmann Production, p. 20; © European Space Agency, p. 21; Xinhua/RIA Xinhua News Agency/Newscom, p. 23; NASA/ESA/Jesse Carpenter/Bill Moede, p. 25; © TARSO SARRAF/AFP/Getty Images, p. 28; Warner Bros. Pictures/Courtesy Everett Collection, p. 30; © European Space Agency/J.Mai, p. 31; NASA, pp. 34, 37, 38, 44, 52 (bottom); © Mark Greenberg/Virgin Galactic/Getty Images, p. 35; © Independent Picture Service, pp. 46, 50; © Jonathan Missel/Texas A&M, p. 47; © Science and Society/SuperStock, p. 52 (top); Rlandmann/Wikimedia Commons (CC BY-SA 3.0), p. 53 (top); Константин Кудинов/Wikimedia Commons (CC BY-SA 3.0), p. 53 (bottom).

Front cover: © NASA/SuperStock.

# About the Author

Karen Romano Young has dived to the bottom of the Pacific Ocean in a tiny submarine; crunched through Arctic ice in an icebreaker; and visited labs, museums, and research institutions across the United States to write and illustrate books about science. She is a lead science communications fellow aboard the research ship *Nautilus*.

She has written and/or illustrated more than thirty books for young readers and is the creator of *Humanimal Doodles,* a science comic. Her nonfiction books include *Try This!* and *Try This Extreme!* Her fiction work includes *The Beetle and Me: A Love Story,* the graphic novel *Doodlebug: A Novel in Doodles,* and *Hundred Percent.*

She lives with her family in the Connecticut woods. She has not yet traveled to space.